How This Book Is Organized

PART 1 HOLLYWOOD VERSUS THE BIBLE

This section is a response to the harmful, insulting, and erroneous views being propagated by Hollywood concerning Angels in movies, on television and in music.

PART 2 THE TRUTH ABOUT ANGELS

This section includes short, theological responses to many of the most damaging and misunderstood ideas and beliefs about Angels. This section will provide in depth answers to the most asked questions about Angels.

PART 3 ANGEL FACTS

This section provides fact based outlines that can be used to teach others the truth about Angels, including the purpose for Angels, the creation of Angels, and the hierarchy of Angels and Demons.

DEDICATION

    I dedicate this book to my sister Tina who is my hero, to my brother Marty who is a wonderful example of what being a United States Marine is all about, to my Mom Stella for "hanging in there and refusing to quit despite life's hard knocks," to my nephews Isaiah, Isaac, and Israel who have been a constant source of inspiration, to Momma Theda and Lisa Mahler for inspiring me to work hard, to take responsibility, and to seek God, and to my cousins Rodney and Denise for watching over me and arming me with truth and knowledge –you are my best friends. Most of all, I want to dedicate this book back to God who saved my life when I was a lost, hurting, and confused teenager who needed a true and faithful Father.

FORWARD

Having known Tracy Lewis for over 15 years, I can attest to her commitment to Christ and her godly character. Her passion for the things of the Lord parallels her love of the Scriptures and her desire to share its timeless truths. With a background in church and parachurch ministry, I heartily commend this work to you.

Diane J. Chandler, Ph.D., Assistant Professor,
School of Divinity, Regent University

This book is an attempt to spread the truth about God's Angels as well as their reality! As a Theologian, former Youth Pastor, and student of the Greek and Hebrew scriptures, I am very protective of God, His Angels, and the Judeo-Christian scriptures all together. I have spent many years and lessons devoting time to teaching the truth about Angels to many people. This book defends the truth about Angels in a straightforward manner and unashamedly debunks Hollywood and the media's most damaging, most insulting, and most erroneous views regarding Angels. Those who read this book will be enlightened and will know the truth about God's magnificently powerful creations. My prayer is that they will, in turn, use this book to teach that truth to others.

Tracy Lewis, Ph.D., MDIV
Principal, Professor

WHAT PEOPLE ARE SAYING

Tracy is a godly woman who is passionate about teaching the truth and helping people grow in their faith. She carries with her a contagious enthusiasm that draws people to God. I am excited to see the impact that this book will make for God's Kingdom.

Tom Hopkins, Pastor
Southpark Community Church, Tulsa OK

"In a day when Reality TV and shows about the paranormal are the norm, it is necessary that Christians stop and consult the Bible about the real nature of angels. Like almost everything else, Hollywood overwhelmingly get this wrong, but somehow the general public, even Christians seem to think that it is acceptable to infuse the Hollywood image of angels into their spiritual beliefs."

Dr. Patrick Otto,
Chair of Graduate Education, Oral Roberts University

If Jesus' time machine had landed him in the fractured and troubled landscape of twenty-first century America instead of in Jerusalem and the Galilee under the Romans, I don't think he could have found a better good-will ambassador for his teachings than Tracy Lewis. She is a persistent encourager in a world that all too often does its best to pull us down, and she has abundant kindness and compassion for others less fortunate.

Herb Beskin, Esquire, Trustee
Law Office, VA

Knowing Tracy Lewis, this book is just the beginning of her journey to an even greater goal. Her lifelong commitment and dedication to God and to defending the Truth has truly been an inspiration to me and my family. No path too long, no goal too high, with a love for God, perseverance, persistence and determination, Tracy Lewis has proven to be a role model for women, both young and old, regardless of their background.

Rodney Hilson, Pastor
Evangelical Baptist Church of Los Angeles, CA

Tracy Lewis is a woman of integrity, kindness, outstanding character and excellence. She embodies the Proverbs 31 woman with her commitment to God, family, friends, colleagues, and community. In addition, she works with purpose, dedication, and passion in everything she endeavors to do.

Marquetta Finley, MS, CPP, Director
Tulsa Community College, OK

CONTENTS

PREFACE

There are many purposes for Angels. Throughout the Bible we see Angels take the form of men and women and walk among us in order to protect us and to communicate the plan of God for us in extraordinary situations. The writer of Hebrews warns us to be kind to strangers because they could be Angels in disguise. Angels stand guard over us to protect us from harm as well as from ourselves, and they even go ahead of us to guide us and watch over us in our journeys in order to bring us to the place God has prepared for us.

In the book of Revelation, we see Angels surrounding the throne of God and crying out with a loud voice that God is worthy to receive praise, honor, glory, strength, wisdom, and power. Here we see the worship of God by myriads of magnificent Angels and their profound reverence before the throne of God as they fall on their faces to worship Him. Angels are devoted to God. Their never-ending praise of God's holiness and majesty is what Angels naturally do.

Praise the Lord, you his angels, you mighty ones who do his bidding, who obey his word (Psalm 103:20 NIV).

Praise him, all his angels, praise him, all his heavenly hosts (Psalm 148:2 NIV).

I

HOLLYWOOD VERSUS THE BIBLE

HOLLYWOOD VS.
THE BIBLE

Angels in the Outfield, Michael, Dogma, The Preacher's Wife, Teen Angel, City of Angels, Constantine, Fallen, and the most recent movie — *Legion* are just a few of the movies about Angels that have been released by Hollywood in the past 15 years. Each of these movies is proof of how very little Hollywood knows about Angels, God, and the Judeo-Christian scriptures. These movies shamefully display Hollywood's disrespect and disdain for anything sacred or Christian, especially God, the Bible, and Angels. It stands to reason that whenever Hollywood attempts to tackle the subject of Angels, BEWARE! They will most assuredly get it wrong.

Hollywood does not understand spiritual matters, which include God, the Bible, Angels, and Demons. They treat them as a joke, or as myths that simply make for good movies and good television. Thus, they make a mockery of the most ancient of texts, the Judeo-Christian scriptures.

The portrayal of Angels in Hollywood movies and on television is almost always wrong and almost always lacking in truth. Hollywood relates to Angels from a purely mortal perspective, a view which is seriously in error. As Hollywood continues to bring Angels down to the same level as humans, they repeatedly portray Angels as flawed, rebellious, corruptible, weak, confused, mortal, etc. Hollywood simply does not know the facts. This ignorance could probably be dispelled if they would simply go to the most reliable and most ancient of texts concerning Angels, the Judeo-Christian scriptures. Alas, this seems to be asking too much of Hollywood. Instead, they keep making it up as they go along, cranking out deceptive movie after movie, which people take to heart and believe as truth.

What follows is a list of some of Hollywood's most popular and most damaging movies about Angels that have been released over the years. While some of these movies may seem harmless, their content is not! Even the most loveable of movies, such *as It's a Wonderful Life* and *The Preacher's Wife,* portray Angels in a negative light. This section debunks these movies as well as Hollywood's worst of the worst in movies about Angels that have been released over the years, all of which I purposely watched for the sake of this writing. Afterwards, you will be presented with the Truth about Angels according to what most scholars consider to be the foremost authority on Angels, the Judeo-Christian scriptures, also known as the Bible.

While I do not have an axe to grind against any one person in particular, I do have an axe to grind against Hollywood in general, an entity which continues to produce one insulting movie and television show after another about Angels, ignoring the facts and deceiving generations of people.

Let's get started!

ANGELS IN MOVIES

IT'S A WONDERFUL LIFE (1946)

This film is Director Frank Capra's inverted take on, *A Christmas Carol*. It stars Jimmy Stewart as George Bailey, a good man who's spent a lifetime giving up on his dreams in order to keep life in his small town humming. When a guardian angel named Clarence finds a despondent George poised to jump off a bridge, he shows George what life would've been like had he never been born (Netflix).

As a fan of the cinema and of Jimmy Stewart, I have to say that this is one of my favorite movies. However, as a Theologian, I must honestly observe that this movie is so far from the truth in its portrayal of the Angel Clarence that I have to include it in my debunking. While this movie is not notoriously and overtly insulting, some things still need to be clarified concerning Angels.

In an effort to help the Angel Clarence get his "wings," God sends Clarence to earth to earn his wings by watching over George Bailey. The real issue with this movie is this: the Angel in this movie is portrayed as a man, who once died and afterwards became an Angel. He is a junior Angel in training; an Angel who needs to earn his wings in order to make it into Heaven and score points with God.

First off, Angels do not have to "earn their wings" or "do good deeds" to get into Heaven. Heaven is already their home. It is the only home Angels have ever known. Secondly, and this fact will surely be most disturbing to the world and to Christians, but *people do not become Angels when they die*. Right now, someone may be tempted to drop this book, but please hang in there and bear with me. This truth needs to be told. Angels are an entirely different class of beings. There are humans and there are Angels. While Angels take the form of humans temporarily while on earth, they are not human, and humans are not in the class of Angels who were created by God before the creation of mankind. The next section of this book will go into more detail regarding this truth for those of you asking, "Where does the Bible say that?"

Finally, the book of Isaiah describes Angels known as *the Seraphim.* These Angels are described as possessing human forms and having wings, however the point needs to be made that these Angels continuously reside over the throne of God. This is their position in Heaven. Artistic drawings and paintings over the years have portrayed all Angels as possessing wings. In actuality, the messenger and ministerial Angels of God who go back and forth between Heaven and earth do not have or need wings. Wings represent flight; therefore people believe that wings are what enable Angels to fly—again, not true. Angels are able to move faster than the speed of light, and do so without the aid of wings. Angels are spirits, and they live in the realm of the spirit, outside of space and time as we humans know it. This enables them to move unhindered and unencumbered through the air. In light of this, wings would only prove weighty and burdensome to an Angel trying to move at the speed of light.

Angels in the Outfield (1994)

This movie is a remake of the 1951 movie of the same name. A young boy named Roger lives in a foster home along with his best friend J.P., but when Roger's dad comes to visit him, a little bit of hope grows back in Roger's heart about him going to live with his dad. But his hopes suddenly die when his dad says that they can be a family again when Roger's favorite baseball team, the California Angels, win the pennant, but the team is currently in last place in their division. So Roger prays to Heaven and asks if the Angels up there can help the California Angels baseball team win the pennant so that Roger can have the family that he always wanted. Because of his prayer, Roger gets what he prays for (imdb.com).

This movie is considered a classic; a heart touching family movie. While it did not stray too far from the truth, and it did not insult the very nature of Angels, a few things still need to be corrected. After the little boy Roger prays to God, Angels arrive on the scene to help. While it is not unlikely that God would send Angels to help a baseball team win a game, it is essential that people remember that we as humans are NOT to worship Angels. Angels are not a support for us to pray to or worship. This is backwards and contrary to God's purpose for Angels. The scriptures tell us that the Angels of God are servants for those who are heirs of salvation, and that Angels go ahead of us to guard us on our journeys (Hebrews 1:14, Exodus 23:20). Angels are devoted servants of God, who will always point us and guide us back to God.

Michael (1996)

This movie is about an Angel (John Travolta) who sees life in Heaven as a burden and a punishment. He comes to earth to do some last minute partying before having to surrender to a lifetime of servitude in Heaven. For Michael, there's no such thing as sin, so during his time on earth, Michael dives headfirst into debauchery—smoking and drinking—while simultaneously attempting to lead a group of reporters, who are unconvinced that he is an Angel (gee, go figure), to redemption.

In the movie *Michael,* Hollywood attempts to do away with the very idea of sin and judgment. The writers of the movie *Michael* are basically saying to people "if an Angel can do it, then it must not be wrong!" While I will not argue as to whether or not smoking and drinking are sins, I will state that they are destructive substances that often lead to life threatening habits and lifestyles, such as death! Smoking causes cancer, and excessive alcohol consumption causes liver failure and has been shown to amplify the cancer-causing activity of other known chemicals, such as tobacco. Excessive drinkers have an increased risk for head and neck cancers, breast cancer and liver cancer. None of which affect Angels! Cancer and liver failure will not harm an Angel. Why? Because Angels are not human!

Angels are heavenly beings who do not live with the everyday temptations of humans. They do not see smoking, drinking and sexual debauchery as fun. On the contrary, Angels have been watching humans fall victim to the same destruction wrought by the abuse of these substances and indulgences since the beginning of time.

Angels are sent to earth for a reason, by God, and with a purpose. Ultimately, they return to their home in Heaven. They do not have to live with the consequences of actions such as drinking, smoking, and sexual immorality. Angels do not have earthly bodies that suffer the effects of sin. These are the vices of humans. Angels make their home in Heaven, where such things do not exist.

THE PREACHER'S WIFE (1996)

In the movie, *The Preachers Wife,* Denzel Washington plays an Angel named Dudley who is sent to earth to aid a preacher and his wife. We find out early on in the movie that Dudley was once a human being who died at a young age; afterwards, he became an Angel, waiting around Heaven for his chance to be sent back to earth. He finally gets this chance and arrives on earth armed with a "handbook for Angels," which he consults whenever he is confused about what an Angel is allowed to do or say. Whitney Houston plays the preacher's wife who is tempted to fall in love with Dudley while Courtney B. Vance plays the busy preacher who never has time for his wife and son. The movie is funny and touching at the same time.

I actually went to the movie theatre in 1996 to see this movie, and I have often noticed that it is a classic holiday movie on the shelves of many people, Christians especially. I am not going to dispute the fact that Angels are dispatched by God to help mankind in times of need. This is true. God does indeed dispatch Angels to aid His people when they call out to Him. In the book of Daniel, Angels are dispatched as soon as Daniel prays, but they are held up and hindered by demons. The Angels wage war with these demons (Fallen Angels) in order to get to Daniel to bring him the answer and deliverance he seeks (Daniel 10:7-14). What I will dispute however, is the movie writer's belief that human beings become Angels of God once they die. This is the most damaging and most widely spread untruth about Angels circulating "rapidly" today, through the mediums of movies, television, and music.

God created the Heavens, the Earth, Angels, and the human race, each for a specific purpose. While Angels temporarily assume the form of humans, they are not human. They are an entirely different class of beings than humans.

CITY OF ANGELS (1998)

This movie is a remake of the 1987 foreign film, *Wings of Desire,* which was applauded by critics as a great film (imdb.com). *City of Angels* has been considered by many people to be one of the most romantic movies of all time. The movie focuses on an Angel named Seth (Nicolas Cage) who has the ability to read human thoughts. Seth watches on as Maggie, a doctor (Meg Ryan) loses a patient in surgery. Afterward, Seth falls in love with Maggie. Seth the Angel is so taken with Maggie that he debates whether to turn in his wings for life as a mortal.

Romanticism aside, this movie again attempts to bring Angels down to the same level as humans. Angels are spiritual beings who reside in the heavenly realms worshipping before the throne of God. Their job is to serve God and to serve humans. Apparently, for Hollywood, this is not an exciting enough life for Angels. No, they have to imagine Angels entangled in the same situations and struggling with the same problems as men and women on earth.

Angels however, are not enticed and led astray by the same sensual pleasures as humans, and they are not sitting around Heaven envying human beings and longing to fall in love with men and women on earth. Angels, unlike humans, are not sexual beings. While Angels do show emotions such as joy, kindness, compassion, and concern they are not sensual or sexual beings. "Though we read of the sons of God we never read of the sons of angels" (Duffield & Van Cleave, 1987). Jesus himself said that the Angels of God do not marry and do not reproduce (Lk.20:34-36).

Lastly, Angels cannot read peoples minds! While in the movie the Angel Seth has the ability to read the thoughts of people, in reality this is impossible for Angels to do. More will be said about this later, but let me say this now—Only God is omniscient (all-knowing), and only He can read the minds' of people. This is a quality which only God possesses! Hollywood is obviously unaware of this.

DOGMA (1999)
Exiled to Wisconsin, a fallen angel named Bartleby (Ben Affleck) and the Angel of Death named Loki (Matt Damon) discover a portal back to Heaven. The portal however is in New Jersey, so they begin a cross-country trek in which they cross

paths with several characters, including a foul demon and a coarse, offensive apostle who walk among humans, fighting for their fate. In Smith's Dogma, an abortion clinic worker receives her higher calling from two clueless prophets who send her on a journey which begins a modern-day battle against evil.

This movie is the worst of the worst when it comes to Angel movies! It tempts one to pray for lightening to strike Kevin Smith. But alas, our duty requires us to pray for him. He needs it.

Dogma deliberately slaps God, Christians, and the church in the face as it attempts to make a mockery of and single-handedly destroy any and all things that Christianity has held sacred. The writer/director of this movie, Kevin Smith, intends to provide a comedic portrayal of Angels in this movie, as well as his take on religion. The result is foul-mouthed Angels who spew profanity and curse everything from God to man. Kevin Smith has a serious axe to grind in this movie, with not only the Catholic Church but with Christianity as a whole. In the movie he portrays God as a playful woman child (singer, Alanis Morisette). While he perpetrates a faith in God in this movie, he knows absolutely nothing whatsoever about God. Smith's faith in this movie is clearly Agnostic and purposeless. Smith wants God, but God without the Bible; he wants God, but without the boundaries that God sets; he wants God, minus the holiness. Smith even ventures to show a battle between good and evil in this movie, which is a surprise. He pushes away the absolutes of God in order to create his own, which makes one wonder what standard of measurement he uses to discern good from evil.

The Angels in the movie Dogma are profane creatures in human form. They curse everything even though, in reality, God's Angels would never curse God! The Angels of God stand before the throne of God daily worshipping God and are blameless before God. Angels are obedient messengers of God who speak only what God instructs them to speak.

Dogma again brings Angels down to the level of man, making those who curse God and partake in all kinds of destructive actions feel good about themselves. "Why feel guilty, or wrong? Surely, if Angels can do it, then it must be okay," is the message that comes through loud and clear in this movie.

Next, there's the abortion clinic worker who gets a higher calling from God through the medium of two clueless prophets. One of Smith's prophets seems to revel in vulgarity for shock value. The other prophet never speaks, until the very end of the movie. The word prophet means "orator." What good is a prophet who never speaks? Let this be a wake-up call to Hollywood! Anyone who functions in the role of a prophet does not wander the streets looking for people to speak words from God to. Besides, anyone who would listen to them would be a fool! Prophets first and foremost must confess a faith in Jesus Christ, and they should minister in a church and to the church body. Prophets are not clueless as to who they are and what they are supposed to do like the prophets in Smith's *Dogma*.

While this movie is probably intended to be a funny portrayal of Angels and demons, it is an utter insult to God, Christianity and to everything holy. Enough said.

Angels in America (2003)

The premise of this movie was that God abandoned Heaven, leaving the Angel of death to take its toll on mankind through the use of AIDS. An Angel (Emma Thompson) appears to an AIDS afflicted man named Prior. The Angel informs Prior that he is a prophet chosen by God to save the world and himself. It also focuses on several characters who have AIDS and who wrestle with coming out of the closet (homosexuality) (Netflix).

Prophets do not wander around aimlessly speaking "thus sayeth the Lord" to the average person on the street. People should take care to be wary of any such person. Prophets are men or women who serve in a ministerial position in Christian churches. Their purpose is to minister to the men and women in congregational settings.

Angels are not independent thinkers! They do not act on their own—believe it or not. They are messengers of God who are sent forth to do God's will (Psalm 103:20). The fact that God would send an Angel as a messenger to a man dying of AIDS should be enough to show that God did not abandon mankind, leaving them to be ravished by death. In other words, the premise of the movie and its plot contradict one another.

God is not the author of AIDS. God is not the author of death. He is not the author of any sickness or disease. God is the author of Life. Jesus said, *"The thief comes only to steal and kill and destroy; I have come that they may have life, and have it to the full"* (John 10:10). People who are sick, hurting, or facing death, and people who are not aware of these words of Jesus, often blame God in the face of sickness, disease, and suffering. The real culprit however crouches down and hides behind the death and destruction of God's most holy creation, mankind.

Mankind is God's most glorious creation. The Bible says that God's ears are attentive to the prayers of the righteous. Who are the righteous? They are the ones who believe in God and confess Jesus Christ as Lord and Savior (Romans 3:1-25). While this is a requirement for those who wish to commune with God, Spirit to spirit, God does send people across the paths of those who do not know Jesus in order to establish a relationship with those who are searching, lost, or crying out to Him for help.

Hollywood wants God without the Bible. Even though God says that mankind, both male and female are God's most precious creation, this is not the message that is preached in these movies. As I said before, Hollywood is ignorant of what the Bible has to say about God, God's Angels, and God's love for all of mankind.

CONSTANTINE (2005)

John Constantine (Keanu Reeves) was a human who tried to commit suicide, but was saved from death, endued with supernatural powers, and then sentenced to spend the rest of his life trying to redeem himself by exorcising demons and sending them back to hell. Constantine can see spirits, both demons and Angels, walking the earth disguised as humans. He is appointed by God to be an earthly Guardian Angel. Constantine teams up with a police detective (Rachel Weisz) to save humanity. He endows her with the same supernatural ability to see spirits so the two of them can fight against both demons and Angels (Netflix).

Constantine's mission on earth is to make sure people earn God's love through suffering and tribulation. A line from *Constantine* says, "If sweet, sweet God loves you so, then I will make you worthy of His love." This movie has a dangerously sad and destructive message. It leads people to believe that they have to earn God's love and favor. This is a lie! *God's love cannot be earned; it is a gift from God and there is nothing we can do to earn it because it is freely given to men and women (Eph. 2:8-9).* This movie in many ways is the most damaging of all movies about Angels in that it tells people that they are not good enough for God to love them. God is not a sadist who feels the need to torture people in order to show them love, as this movie would have viewers believe.

The other deception propagated in this movie is that people who die return to earth as Angels. As stated earlier, this is the biggest misunderstanding about Angels circulating today. Angels are an entirely different race of beings. They are not humans (Lk. 24:37). They temporarily assume the form of humans to fulfill their purpose on the earth, but they then return to their home in Heaven. When a human dies, their spirit either returns to God or is sent to Hell, depending on their confession of faith. There is no returning to earth; no second chance!

FALLEN (2006)

This movie was billed as a family movie. It was about an Angel whose mission was to redeem fallen Angels and return them to Heaven. This movie is flawed and wrong in that fallen Angels cannot be redeemed. There is no redemption for them. Fallen Angels (demons) have been judged by God and His judgment is final (2 Pet 2:4, Jude 6).

Heaven is a paradise; a wonderful, reality that exist beyond space and time as we limited humans are able to experience and know it. Angels are not going AWOL and jumping ship to leave Heaven to come to earth. The Angels in Heaven rebelled once, before the creation of mankind. The rebels, Lucifer and his fallen angel cohorts, were kicked out of Heaven by Michael the Archangel. This was the only time in the history of God's creation that Angels of God were stripped of their holiness. It was also the only occurrence of an Angel rebellion, and was witnessed by Jesus Christ himself who said, "I saw Satan fall like lightning from heaven" (Luke 10:18).

The portrayal of Angels repeatedly sinning against God is a lie that is perpetuated by Hollywood. As stated earlier, what could an Angel possibly want on earth? Nothing! They are not tempted by sin like men and women, and they are not ruled by sensuality or by greed. More will be said about this later on.

LEGION (2009)

In Hollywood's newest Angel flick, "Legion," a diner in the middle of nowhere becomes the battleground for the survival of the human race for a group of trapped strangers. The premise in this movie is that God has lost faith in humans; therefore, he sends his *legion of Angels* to start the Apocalypse and to destroy the entire human race. Mankind's only hope lies in a rebel Angel who, aware of God's plan, rebels against God and shows up at the diner (in a car) to defend and fight with the humans against God's legion of Angels.

Believe it or not, God actually loves his creation, mankind. The Bible tells us that God has a purpose and plan for every man and woman, and it is for good, not evil (Jeremiah 29:11). God himself declares in Malachi, *"I the Lord do not change"* (3:8), and the apostle James tells us, *"Don't be deceived, my dear brothers. Every good and perfect gift is from above, coming down from the Father of the heavenly lights, who does not change like shifting shadows. He chose to give us birth through the word of truth, that we might be a kind of first fruits of all he created"* (James 1:16-18 NIV). The apostle Peter also tells us that God is patient with us (mankind) and does not want any of us to perish, but he wants everyone to come to repentance (2 Pet. 3:9b). If these words are true, and they are, God does not change his mind concerning his most cherished creation.

God is not chomping at the bit to obliterate us. He will not just send His Angels willy nilly to wipe out the human race. It is contradictory for God to suddenly "change his mind" as the movie *Legion* proposes. This again is an example of Hollywood viewing God and Angels from a purely human perspective, a perspective that is marred by hatred, judgment, and intolerance for men and women, whom they deem unworthy of God's love.

In the movie *Legion* we hear that "God is mad at his children" and "God has lost faith in man." What a nasty representation of God. God is the superlative of love. Even when humans lose faith in other humans, God does not. He is able to love, even when people are unlovable, hateful, and forgiving. This in and of itself is enough to counter this disgusting movie. Who do these writers think they are?

ANGELS ON TELEVISION

Is it too much to ask for Hollywood to get it right! Obviously it is. It is apparent that they are not interested in perpetuating the truth and getting their Angel facts straight. Of course not, television would be too boring.

Before the 1980s, Angels were not talked about much in the church, or in books, films, and music. However, television shows like *Highway to Heaven* and *Touched by an Angel* in the 1980s touched off a hail storm in Hollywood and Angels were thrust into the Hollywood spotlight. The ensuing result of Hollywood's portrayal of God's Holy Angels has gone from bad to worse ever since.

Hollywood's depiction of Angels has been blasphemous (yes, people still use that word), insulting, degrading, crude, and downright wrong. The Judeo-Christian scriptures are the foremost recognized authority on Angels. These scriptures pinpoint the creation of Angels as preceding the creation of the earth, as well as the fall of Satan and a third of the Angels from Heaven. All other references to Angels in pagan lore or other ancient civilizations' texts postdate the Judeo-Christian scriptures. Therefore, it is to these sacred texts that I will refer when discussing and arguing the facts and truth concerning Angels.

People may say, "What's the big deal? It's only a movie," or "It's only a song. I don't really care about the words." However, there are millions of people who do take it seriously and as the gospel truth. I continuously encounter people who base their ideologies and beliefs about Angels on what they have seen and heard in movies, on television, and in music, and they honestly believe these things to be true. Since these false teachings about Angels have been spreading like wildfire for over 20 years now, it is time to address the most harmful of these lies.

Angels are NOT myths! Hollywood is spreading this lie through movies and television. People are categorizing Angels in the same category as Cyclops, Hercules, and the gods and goddesses of Greek mythology, and in the same category as our more modern myths, Santa Claus and the Easter Bunny. To a lot of people, Angels are just wishful thinking. Keep in mind that many of the writers in Hollywood who propagate such teachings are atheists or agnostics, so their beliefs come as no surprise. However, for those who call themselves Christians, such a belief is perilous to one's faith.

The 1990s and the new millennium era of television has ushered in an even bigger fascination with Angels and demons in television. An anti-biblical and ungodly wave of shows is portraying Angels in roles that are completely opposite their true nature. Week after week, spread across television and streamed across the internet into millions of homes, these televised shows perpetuate deceptive lies about Angels and strip them of their glorious nature, bringing them down to the level of flawed and sinful mortal humans.

Let's start with the worst of the worst!

SUPERNATURAL

Brothers Sam and Dean Winchester investigate all the spooky mysteries that come their way as they travel the country in search of their missing father. Using clues from Dad's journal, the boys traverse the lonely back roads in their 1967 Chevy Impala, encountering numerous otherworldly entities. Sam searches for a way to save Dean from the bargain he made—his soul in exchange for Sam's life. And as the war against the demons draws near, the brothers continue to investigate paranormal events as they confront their roles as saviors of mankind (Netflix).

This television show is the worst of the worst on television! On a recent episode of this show, lead actor Jensen Ackles' character "Dean" states, "The Bible gets more things wrong, than it does right." Clearly the producers and actors of *Supernatural* have, like so many, approached the Bible from a purely godless and secular point of view. They, like the majority of Hollywood, have no knowledge of God or the scriptures; therefore they view the Judeo-Christian Bible as a myth, and see no harm in trashing it! If this were the Koran, I am sure they would think twice out of fear for their lives. Many Christians however, rest quietly in the knowledge that God's Word is the highest form of reality that exists.

This show is a slap in the face to God and to Christians. The producers of this hate-filled show hide behind the fact that they are Jewish and Catholic, like it makes a difference! Even the actors claim to come from wholesome Christian homes. I fail to understand how a Christian could possibly prefer to insult God and His Angels on a weekly basis using derogatory comments that will not be repeated in this book. These actors might as well refer to themselves as Atheists or Agnostics because in similar fashion, they treat God, Angels and demons on this show as simple mythology. Moreover, Jesus Christ on this show is a simple profane utterance used at will by the writers and actors.

SAVING GRACE

Saving Grace focuses on the life of a woman named Grace, a self-destructive police detective who hits bottom after a drunken driving accident. This incident propels her into asking for guidance. Her plea is answered by a quirky Angel named Earl, who offers to help steer her back onto a healthy course. No easy task, considering Grace's life has become a complete shambles (Netflix).

The fact that this program is in its third year on television shows that people are fascinated by the subject matter: the idea of an Angel watching over and helping to guide a mere mortal woman through life. This premise is a throw back to actor Michael Landon's 1980s show, *Highway to Heaven.*

It is the heart's desire of the human race to feel constantly protected and nurtured, and to have a presence and power larger than us, who can manipulate circumstances in our favor, and protect us from harm, even from ourselves. It is human nature to desire these things, and it is not wrong. This is why television shows of this sort are successful. However (and you knew this was coming), Angels would never, ever presume to take the place of God. Angels always point a person back to God. This is why they are assigned to us, and why they appear among us, for brief periods of time (Heb. 13:2). If Angels were to remain among us for prolonged periods of time, humans would begin to worship them. As it stands, once their task is complete, the Angels of God quickly return to where they came from: Heaven.

This show, like so many of Hollywood's films, again brings Angels down to the level of mortal mankind. The Angel Earl in this television show chews tobacco and drinks beer. While these habits are not necessarily sinful, they are nonetheless life threatening, self-destructive habits in and of themselves. While these are vices encouraged by demons for the destruction of human bodies, God's Angels would never perpetuate such an abusive lifestyle.

TEEN ANGEL

Having expired after eating a bad hamburger, a teenage boy named Marty is appointed his best friend Steve's Guardian Angel (Netflix).

While reincarnation is a belief in some cultures, it is not consistent with Judeo-Christian teachings. The book of Hebrews says, "Just as man is destined to die once, and after that to face judgment" (9:27). This means there is no coming back once you die, in any form, be it an Angel or an animal. It doesn't happen. While it is comforting to believe that our family and friends are always with us as Angels on earth watching over us, it is not true. The scriptures tell us that to be absent from our bodies is to be present with the Lord (2 Cor. 5:8). When we die, our spirits immediately return to God or descend into Hell, depending on our confession, or lack thereof.

Humans do not become Angels when they die. This is the most erroneous and most popular untruth about Angels. While a Guardian Angel may have been watching over Steve in this movie, it was not Marty. Angels are an entirely different class of beings.

ANGELS IN MUSIC

The common misconception that people and Angels are the same began spreading like wildfire in the early 1990s through the mediums of music, movies, and television. Classic songs from the 1950s and 1960s, like *Angel* by Elvis Presley and *Earth Angel* by the Penguins, told the world through song that their girlfriends were actually angels. This false, heretical view of Angels has continued over the decades and even in modern day songs such as *Angel* by Jon Secada, *How Could an Angel Break My Heart* by Toni Braxton, *"Angel of Mine,"* by Monica, *"I Need an Angel,"* by Ruben Studdard and other singers such as Shaggy, Pig, Aerosmith, Madonna, Timbuk 3, Hinder, and the Dave Matthews Band. These musicians and their songs have served to mislead and misguide generations of people regarding the nature of Angels.

Many singers insult and desecrate the image of God's Holy Angels by describing their romantic or sexual partners as Angels in disguise. These artists are plagued by an abundance of ignorance when it comes to the Angels of God, and their beliefs are completely opposite what is taught about Angels in the Bible. *While Angels temporarily take the form of men and women, Angels are not sensual creatures; they do not marry, and they do not procreate* (Lk. 20:36). Angels also show emotions (Hebrews 1:14; Luke 15:10), however, they do not engage in sexual relations with humans.

While the list of singers who violate the sanctity of the nature of Angels in their music is ongoing, there are a handful of singers who have managed to get it right and express the true nature of Angels in their music. Sarah McLaughlin for example, in her soft ballad, *In the Arms of the Angel* and Alabama's spiritual country song, *"Angels Among Us."*; former X-Rated rapper, DMX (who is now a born-again Christian) also gets it right in his song entitled, *Angel.* Unfortunately, the list of those who get it right is slim! Whether rock, pop, country, or soul, there are more singers out there who get it wrong than get it right!

II

THE TRUTH ABOUT ANGELS

ANGEL QUIZ

1. Do people become Angels when they die?
2. Are Angels chubby naked babies?
3. Are Michael the Archangel and Jesus Christ one and the same?
4. Is Satan a Fallen Angel?
5. Do Angels have bodies like humans?
6. Are there more Angels than there are people?
7. Can Angels reproduce?
8. Can you kill an Angel?
9. Are children assigned guardian Angels to watch over them?
10. Can Angels go to hell?
11. Will Christians one day judge Angels?
12. Can Angels assume the form of men and women and walk among us on earth?
13. Do Angels live among us on earth most of the time?
14. Can Angels express emotions?
15. Do Angels live inside of and possess humans?

If you do not know the answers to these questions, yet you desire to, then I suggest you continue reading. The answers to each of these questions will be answered as you read the rest of this book.

ANGELS ARE STRONG AND POWERFUL

Let it be known that Angels are not weak, timid, or vulnerable, and they are most definitely not little "fat naked babies." How could anyone believe in the mighty presence and power of Angels to protect them with this image in their mind? While babies are most assuredly both innocent and helpless, Angels are NOT! They are mighty, powerful, and strong.

Movies and television shows such as, *Constantine, City of Angels, Supernatural, Saving Grace, Angel, and Teen Angel* portray God's Angels as mortal, destructible, weak, and vulnerable. Some of these films and shows even go as far as to reduce Angels down to the level of humans by making a joke out of Bible, God, and His Angels. We see shows such as *Supernatural* and *Saving Grace*, which portray Angels struggling with the same emotions and moral dilemmas as humans. Even worse are the movies which portray Angels as angry, vengeful, God haters, or destroyers of mankind. This is NOT the character of Angels, but of demons.

ANGELS ONLY ASSUME HUMAN FORMS

What's wrong with believing that people are Angels? What harm can come from it? While this chapter will surely shock, surprise and upset many people and their preconceived ideas about Angels, the truth must be told.

While there are a number of views regarding Angels in various cultures and even in archaic lore, the Judeo-Christian scriptures contain the earliest, most in-depth teachings about Angels. These scriptures are viewed by evangelicals and Judeo-Christian scholars as the single authority on Angels.

Angels do not have bodies in the sense that humans do. They simply assume human forms. Only on special occasions does God allow people to see Angels, most likely because of the human temptation to worship Angels. Hebrews 13:1-2 commands us to show love to each other, especially to "not forget to entertain strangers, for by so doing some people have entertained Angels without knowing it" (NIV). This key word in verse 2 is "strangers," which brings me to confront a highly propagated misconception about Angels.

With this verse in mind, we need to realize that Angels are not family members, neighbors, or lifelong friends that we have grown up with, known, and loved. Angels are a separate race from the human race. A clear distinction between the class of Angels and the class of humans is made in Hebrews 1:14 and 2:5-8.

ANGELS ARE TOO NUMEROUS TO COUNT

Have you ever wondered how many Angels there are, or how many Angels God created? What about whether or not there are enough Angels to go around for every single person on the face of the earth? Is God creating more Angels every day, or are the same Angels that He created in the beginning still hanging around? The Bible has answers to each of these questions.

Only God knows how many Angels there are, however Hebrews 12:22 says that the Angels of God are "an innumerable company of Angels" (Strong's, 1990, KJV) and that thousands upon thousands of Angels live and rejoice in the heavenly Jerusalem, the city of the living God. Revelation 5:11 also tells us that "Angels, numbering thousands upon thousands, and ten thousand times ten thousand" circle the throne of God singing.

Even though Lucifer (Satan) caused a third of the Angels of God to be cast out of Heaven by the Archangel Michael and his warrior Angels (Rev 12:7-9), an "innumerable company of Angels" remain faithful to God. The word "innumerable" lets us know that there are more than enough Angels to go around! While the number of mankind (male and female) can be numbered on the earth, the Angels of God are innumerable, which means they cannot be counted.

Angels are immortal. They never die! The same angels that were created before the beginning of the world are still serving at the throne of God (Luke 20:36). Of course, Fallen Angels are an exception to this. While Angels are indestructible, the Fallen Angels who rebelled against God before the beginning of the world as we know it were sentenced by God to eternal punishment (Jude 6).

ANGELS HAVE PERSONALITIES AND SHOW EMOTION

Angels are wise, moral beings. They are wise with knowledge that far exceeds that of humans. In the book of Samuel (14:20), Joab compares the wisdom of King David to that of an Angel, and in the book of Matthew, Jesus declares the wisdom of Angels to be above that of men and women (24:36).

Angels know right from wrong. "For if God did not spare angels when they sinned, but sent them to hell, putting them into gloomy dungeons to be held for judgment;" (2 Pet.2:4 NIV), and "the angels who did not keep their positions of authority but abandoned their own home—these he has kept in darkness, bound with everlasting chains for judgment on the great Day" (Jude 6 NIV). These scriptures show the ability of Angels to choose right from wrong. According to Duffield and Van Cleave (1987):

> There was a time of probation during which the angels could choose to obey God or to disobey. Those who disobeyed were cast out, while those who obeyed were confirmed in their stand for God. We do not

*read of any angels falling after the period of proba-
tion ends.* (p.468)

Angels are also capable of showing emotions like joy,
kindness, concern and compassion (Luke 15:10). In the book
of Genesis, the Angels of God take great care to protect Lot
and his family from harm while they are in the city of Sodom.
Moreover, the Angels show kindness and compassion by taking them by their hands and leading them out of the city, and
by making sure they are out of harm's way before destroying
the city of Sodom (Gen. 19:10-22). We are also told that the
Angels of God rejoiced when God made the earth (Job 38:4-7),
and that Angels rejoice when sinners repent (Heb. 1:14, 12:22).
The ability of Angels to show emotions and to possess per-
sonality can be clearly seen in these scriptures.

ANGELS ARE NOT OMNIPRESENT

While Angels are capable of moving from place to place in the blink of an eye, Angels are not *omnipresent*. They are not able to be present everywhere at the same time. They can only be in one place at one time. Omnipresence can only be attributed to God. *God is everywhere at the same time.* Nothing and no one besides God can lay claim to this attribute.

Whereas humans are made up of tangible, relatable matter, Angels are invisible to the human eye the majority of the time (Heb. 13:2; Gen 19:1; Lk. 1: 26; Jn.20:12; Acts 8:26; Acts 12:7). Angels are not corporeal. They do not have bodies that are made up of matter like humans. Angels are spirits. Psalm 104:4 compares Angels to spirits and to flames of fire. Jesus said that a spirit does not have flesh and bones (Lk. 24:37). A spirit is therefore not bound by gravity, time, space or physical obstacles. Angels can move quickly and rapidly, faster than the speed of light, only slowing down to become matter and to become visible to the human eye in order to communicate (as a messenger from God) in an up close and personal way with humans.

When Jesus was born, a great company of Angels appeared to a group of shepherds in a field to announce the birth of the Christ (Lk. 2:13). In the blink of an eye, they appeared. They had been there all along, waiting for the right moment to burst forth in exaltation and to show themselves to the shepherds. The word "company" in Luke 2:23, in military terms, means that the number of Angels who appeared that night was equal to two or three platoons of soldiers. What an unforgettable sight! One moment, the shepherds are enjoying the calm serenity of the open fields with only the bleating of sheep in their ears when suddenly, behold, a company of angels appeared right before them! The shepherds could not help but speak of their encounter. They went into town to spread the news and to look for the baby Jesus. They found the baby in the manger just as the Angels had announced.

I have never asked God to *show me an Angel.* I have always believed that Angels are real. Over the years, I have come to realize that Angels are always present around me to watch over me, and I believe that God can send Angels to guide me like he did Philip in Acts 8:26.

ANGELS ARE NOT OMNISCIENT

While a parallel can be drawn between the ministry of Angels and the ministry of the Spirit of God (the Holy Spirit), let me stress that *Angels are not* omniscient (all-knowing). Although they are wise beings, Angels do not know all things, and they cannot read the minds of people. This ability belongs to God alone. First Peter tells us that there are things that the Angels of God do not know, that they desire to look into (1:12). Matthew also tells us that nobody knows the day or hour of Christ's return, *not even the Angels* of God (24:36).

Angels are not capable of searching the depths of the human spirit. Only the Spirit of God can do this. This truth is affirmed by the Apostle Paul in first Corinthians when he declares: *"For who among men knows the thoughts of a man except the man's spirit within him? In the same way no one knows the thoughts of God except the Spirit of God"* (2:11 NIV). Again and again the Judeo-Christian scriptures speak of God's ability to know and read the thoughts of men and women, both young and old. King David expressed this absolute truth when he spoke concerning God, *"You know when I sit and when I rise; you perceive my thoughts from afar"*

(Psalm 139:2 NIV). Again the scriptures declare, *"...for the Lord searches every heart and understands every motive behind the thoughts"* (I Chr. 28:9 NIV). The Lord even knows the thoughts of the wicked (Psalm 10:4; Prov. 15:26; Isa. 55:7) as well as the thoughts of believers. Other scriptures speak about God's desire to reveal His thoughts to His children (Prov. 1:23; I Cor. 2:16; Heb. 4:12). While the scriptures offer many references to God's ability to read the minds of humans, there are no references to either the Angels of God, or to Fallen Angels ever possessing this attribute or ability.

ANGELS ARE NOT OMNIPOTENT

While Angels are strong and powerful, they are NOT omnipotent. Only God possesses this characteristic. Angels do not have the power to possess or live inside of a person, convict a person of sin, change a person's heart, or regenerate them. Only the Spirit of God is capable of doing these things. He alone is responsible for transforming believers into the image of Christ.

"I am the Lord God Almighty," is a prominent description used by God to identify himself to His people. The people of God, in turn, also described God as "the Almighty God!" The word Almighty in the Hebrew is *"shaddai,"* which means omnipotent, all powerful One. In the Greek the word Almighty is *"pantokrator,"* which means omnipotent, the ruler of all. These words are only used in the scriptures to describe God. In the book of Revelation, a great multitude is heard shouting, *"Alleluia: for the Lord God omnipotent reigns"* (Rev. 19:6 NKJV). While the Angels of God are referred to as powerful in the scriptures (2 Thes. 1:7; 2 Pet. 2:11), the Greek word used in these scripture is *"dunatos,"* which means strong, powerful and capable. Angels are NOT referred to as omnipotent in

the Hebrew and Greek scriptures. Angels receive their orders
and their power from their Creator, God Almighty (the Omnipotent One). *"Praise the Lord, you his angels, you mighty
ones who do his bidding, who obey his word"* (Psalm 103:20
NIV). Only God alone is declared Omnipotent.

ANGELS DO NOT POSSESS HUMANS

Often referred to as demons or devils, Fallen Angels are quite capable of possessing a human body. The New Testament records 33 references to demons and demon-possession whereas the New Testament does not make any references to Angels possessing humans. There are no recorded incidents of Angels ever taking possession of humans or controlling them for either good or evil purposes. There is a reason for this. Simply put, they have no reason to! It is a preposterous joke to think that an Angel would ever NEED to use a human body for anything. They are not tempted by and do not yield to sensual lusts and pleasures like humans do. Moreover, they do not need to possess a human in order to do battle of any kind. They possess enough power on their own.

A human body could not contain the glory of an Angel. They are way too powerful. A human body can barely contain the presence of a demon (Fallen Angel). Demons were stripped of their glory when they were cast out of Heaven before the beginning of creation as we know it. Their sole purpose now is to control and destroy mankind. This is NOT the purpose of Angels.

The Spirit of God (the Holy Spirit) is the only holy entity who is able to fill, live inside of, and take control of a human being. Even so, he does not violate the will of men and women. We have to invite him to come in and live inside of us. Possession is not a suitable word here because it denotes control. God desires that a person willingly surrender control of their lives to Him. He never commands it! Ten references to "being filled with the Spirit of God" can be read in the New Testament. With the Spirit of God living and dwelling inside of you, there is no room for any other spirit. Let me also stress at this point that the ministry of Angels differs from the ministry of the Spirit of God. While the ministry of Angels seems to be especially related to brief, short-lived external matters, the Spirit of God ministers to believers with regard to internal spiritual matters.

In the many cases of demon-possession mentioned in the New Testament, Jesus, the Disciples, Paul, and other named and unnamed Christians were quick to cast out demons from people. Jesus and the early Christians never let a demon stay in possession of one of God's children. The same should hold true today. This book however is not about demons, but about the Angels of God. The ministry of Angels in relation to Christians today, parallels that of the early church. Angels are available and ready to administer protection and deliverance, to strengthen and encourage, and to offer direction and guidance to God's people, from the outside.

ANGELS PROTECT AND FIGHT FOR GOD'S PEOPLE

On judgment day, it will be the Angels of God who will cast the unbelieving and wicked into hell. The book of Daniel vividly illustrates the ongoing battle being waged by Angels in the spirit realm on our behalf. When we pray for help, Angels are at times dispatched in answer to our prayers. When we do not receive our answer right away, Angels are dispatched to fight back Fallen Angels (demons) who are preventing the Angels of God from coming to our aide (Daniel 10:7-14).

Angels are sent by God to protect the children of God. In the book of Exodus, Angels encamped around and went ahead of God's children, protecting them and warning them of impending danger (Ex. 23:20; 32:34; 33:2). "See, I am sending an angel ahead of you to guard you along the way and to bring you to the place I have prepared" (Ex. 23:23 NIV). Psalm 34:7 says "the angel of the Lord encamps around those who fear him and he delivers them." According to Brown, Driver, and Biggs (1979), the word fear in this verse means "those who stand in reverence and awe of the Lord." It is therefore implied here that deliverance and protection is contingent upon a person's reverence and respect for God.

Psalm 91 also tells us how God's Angels will protect his children when they come to him for shelter and protection from danger: *"For he will command his Angels concerning you to guard you in all your ways"* (NIV 91:11). When we make the Most High God (El Olam) our refuge, protection from harm is ready at hand.

In the New Testament, the Angels of God are just as much in the business of protecting God's people as they are in the Old Testament. After Peter and John are thrown into prison, an Angel of the Lord supernaturally opens the doors of the locked jail cell and sets them free. The Angel manages to do this while the prison guards stand watch at the doors. Afterwards, an Angel tells the apostles to *"Go, stand in the temple courts, and tell the people the full message of this new life"* (Acts 5:20). When the chief priests send to the jail for the Peter and John, they find the jail cell empty. Everyone is shocked and confused! The Captain of the Temple Guard has no answer for how the Apostles escaped, so he is subsequently executed.

While many of us may never experience being beaten and locked up in a jail cell, we can still see and experience God's deliverance in our lives. Having driven across the United States several times and back, I have experienced firsthand the delivering power of God, enough to know that Angels are indeed a reality, not a myth! From the East Coast to the West Coast, up the West Coast across Canada to Alaska, and back again, I have encountered many perilous situations, but I was delivered from them through the interception of Angels. I take great comfort in knowing that God's Angels do indeed watch over me. Psalm 91 is true every day of my life, and in the lives of my friends and family. In the face of adversity and danger, the Angels of God are present, willing, and able to deliver us all. *"The righteous face many troubles, but the LORD rescues them from each and every one"* (Psalm 34:19 NLT).

Angels Escort Our Spirits to Heaven

Angels escort the souls of humans into Heaven after death (Lk. 16:22). When Lazarus the beggar died, the Angels of God escorted him into Abraham's bosom (this phrase in the Greek indicates "into a place of honor" or "into paradise"). This is a somewhat overlooked ministry of Angels, but it can be of comfort to those who are near death. Many people have testified, at the moment of their departure from this life, of being conscious of the presence of heavenly Angels around them (Duffield & VanCleave, 1987).

MY ANGEL ENCOUNTER

The sight of an Angel in all its splendor and glory can be a terrifying sight to mere mortals. Whenever an Angel appeared to men and women in the Bible, people fell to their knees in fear and out of reverence for the majestic creature standing before them. Then the Angel would almost always say to the man or woman, "Do not be afraid!"

Let me go on record and say, I have never, ever asked to see an Angel. While some people may say, "I need to see in order to believe," I don't. I know Angels are real. Not only do I take God's word for it, but I have had enough close encounters of my own in my lifetime to convince me that Angels are real. In my travels to several countries, and to 47 states, my life has been spared countless times as a result of Angel intervention. I will share one of these moments with you.

After 10 days in Australia, and changing planes three times on the way back home, my plane finally landed in Norfolk. I was exhausted, and the only thing I could think of was food, home and sleep. Unfortunately, I lived three hours north in Charlottesville. I had parked at my dad's house in Virginia Beach, in order to fly out of Norfolk. My dad was waiting for me at the airport to drive me back to his house. When we arrived, my stepmom Joann was waiting for us with dinner ready. As we all sat down to eat, I shared stories from my latest trip *down under*. It was late and dark outside when I finally set out on the road home to Charlottesville. I had a three hour drive ahead of me. As always, I prayed for traveling grace and for the Angels of God to watch over me as I drove along the road. Normally, this would be a short, relaxing drive for me, but I was weary from my trip and trying hard to stay awake. I turned the music up in an effort to distract myself from the exhaustion. I could have stayed overnight at my dad's and waited until morning to make the drive home. But after two weeks in a hotel and riding on airplanes, I was determined to sleep in my own bed that night. Soon enough, I approached the Hampton Roads Bridge and proceeded across. There were very few cars on the bridge that night. I was glad. I could set my cruise control and relax.

I saw the Hampton Roads Tunnel approaching in the distance. Although I had driven through it countless times, I hated the tunnel! It made me nervous. It was over a mile long, and it ran under water—which totally freaked me out. It seemed to go on forever, and the bright, fake light along the walls inside always gave me a headache and strained my eyes. However, it spanned the inlet connecting Norfolk and Hampton, so there was no getting around it if I wanted to take the short cut home.

I descended down into the tunnel, trying hard to stay focused and alert. I'll never forget what happened next, for as long as I live. Suddenly, a voice was shouting in my ear, "Wake up"! Startled, I opened my eyes, and let out a loud gasp. I had fallen asleep! Immediately, I sat up and grabbed onto the wheel of my Durango, which was quickly ascending *up out* of the tunnel on the other side into the darkness of Hampton. My heart was pounding out of control as I gripped the wheel. I held onto the wheel for dear life as I drove along the highway. "What just happened?" I kept asking myself, trying to replay the last few minutes in my mind. I opened all of the windows in order to let the cold air rush in.

I could not recall driving through the tunnel at all that night. I did remember hearing the voice shouting to me, "Wake up!" While I found it hard to believe, I knew it had happened. I knew an Angel had saved me that night by guiding my vehicle the entire distance through the tunnel. I believed in Angels before that night, and even more so afterwards. I had prayed Psalm 91 before I left for Australia and believed that "God would give his Angels charge over me and watch over me," and He did. I cried as I thought about what could have happened, but my tears turned to laughter and shouts of joy on the road that night as I thought of God's love for me! Needless to say, I remained awake for the rest of my drive back to Charlottesville.

CONCLUSION

Who could ever believe in the type of Angels that Hollywood creates? In movies and on television, and even in music and pop culture fiction, Angels are portrayed as wimpy, boring, angry, rebellious, human-hating, human possessing, purposeless, powerless beings. Those who portray them as such have clearly never even cracked open the Bible! The Truth is—Angels are none of these things! However, in the name of entertainment, Hollywood continues to recreate Angels in *their* image.

Those faithful to Angelology must continue to defend the truth about Angels, and see Angels as God sees them, as they truly are, magnificent and powerful! Angels are spirits who appear to us in human form, for a short time in response to prayer or in times of trouble. Angels are always sent by God to serve his creation, mankind. Throughout the Bible, from the beginning in the book of Genesis, to the end in the book of Revelation, the Angels of God are actively present in the lives of God's people to aid, guide, protect, and comfort them. In the face of fear and suffering and in times of distress, Angels are all around us, always. We may not see them, but we must believe that they are there, ready to do God's bidding. This is faith.

I often pray for God to send His Angels ahead of me and to watch over me. The most comforting thought to me in the face of persecution and danger, or when I travel is that I am most definitely "not alone." On more than one occasion, Angels have come between trouble and me. As a child of God, this is a part of my inheritance.

III

ANGEL FACTS

THE PURPOSE OF ANGELS

The most important characteristic of Angels is not that they have power to exercise control over our lives, or that they are beautiful, but that they work on our behalf. They are motivated by an inexhaustible love for God and are jealous to see that the will of God in Jesus Christ is fulfilled in us (Billy Graham).

Hebrews 1:14 – *All* Angels are ministering spirits, sent to be servants, in some capacity, to the "heirs of salvation."

Hebrews 13:2; Gen. 18, 19:1-3 - Angels can take the form of men and women and walk among us.

Psalm 103 – Angels respond to the spoken (*rhema*) Word of God.

Exodus 23:20 – Angels go ahead of us to guard us on our journey and to bring us to the place God has prepared for us.

Exodus 23:21, 22; Judges 6:22 – Angels communicate to us the plan of God for us in situations.

Psalm 91; Num.22:23; Ps.34:7 – Angels stand guard over us to protect us, even if it means protecting us from ourselves.

Daniel 8:15ff – Angels fight for us in the spiritual and heavenly realms. When we pray and do not receive what we pray for right away, sometimes Angels have to be dispatched to fight back the enemy in order for us to receive our answers from God.

Matthew 13:49 – The Angels will separate the wicked from the righteous on judgment day and cast the wicked into hell.

FIVE TYPES OF ANGELS

There are five types of Angels in existence:

Ministering Angels (Heb. 1:14; Col. 1:16; 1 Pet. 3:22)

Messenger Angels (Gen. 31:11; Judg. 2:4; 1 Kgs. 19:5; Zec. 1:9; Mt. 1:20, 28:5; Lk. 1:13, 2:10; Acts 27:23). Gabriel, the Mighty One stands out in the Bible and is one of the only two Angels to be mentioned by name. He appeared to Mary in Nazareth, and to Daniel in Babylon (Dn.8:15ff; 9:20ff; Lk. 1:13, 19, 26-38).

Michael (referred to as Michael the Archangel and the Prince of Princes). Michael, like Gabriel, stands out among all of the other Angels. Michael is the only other Angel in the Bible who is mentioned by name (Dn.12:1; 10:13, 21; Jude 9; 1Thes. 4:16).

Cherubim – painted and woven into the art of the Ark, the holy of holies, and the temple (Gen.3:24; Exo.37:6-9; 2 Kgs.19:15; Exo.26:1; Rev.4:5-6, 14)

Seraphim – stands above the throne of God (Isa. 6:6-7)

OFFICES OF ANGELS AND DEMONS

According to the Bible (Eph. 1:21; Col. 1:16; 1 Pet. 3:22), there are five different offices of authority among Angels:

1. Thrones
2. Dominions
3. Principalities
4. Authorities
5. Powers

While the offices of Angels are clear in the scriptures, the purpose for and designation of such offices is not as clear. Moreover, in comparison to the offices of authority among Angels, are the positions of authority that exists among devils.

Ephesians 6:12 says the Christian's struggle in this world is not against humans, flesh and blood, but against the following devils:

1. Spiritual Forces of Evil in the Heavenly Realms
2. Powers
3. Authorities
4. Rulers

Hell was prepared by God for Satan and his demons. (Matt. 25:41). Putting on the whole armor of God is the only thing that we as Christians can use to take our stand against demonic forces. Standing firm in the truth, and in righteousness, with the Word of God and faith, and by praying in the Spirit on all occasions are our weapons. The Apostle John wrote that *everyone who is born of God overcomes the world, and the victory that has overcome the world is our faith* in the fact that Jesus is the Son of God (1 Jn. 5:6).

THE PLACE OF ANGELS IN THE ORDER OF CREATION

The book of Colossians tells us that *"For by him all things were created: things in heaven and on earth, visible and invisible, whether thrones or powers or rulers or authorities; all things were created by him and for him."* The phrase "thrones or powers or rulers or authorities" refers to the Angels of God and the rank or order which they hold. Psalm 148:2-5 also tells us that all of the heavenly hosts, meaning Angels, were created by God. These scriptures declare God (Elohim) to be the creator of all of the Angels.

In Genesis we see God creating the heavens. Colossians 1:16 tells us that the Angels of God were created along with the creation of the heavens. The book of Job states that "the Angels of God shouted for joy when God created the earth" (Job 38:4-7 NIV). This scripture enables us to place the creation of Angels as predating the creation of the earth.

After creating the earth, God then creates the human race (male and female). It is to these humans that God sends His Angels as messengers, protectors, guardians, and servants. The book of Hebrews declares that all Angels have been sent to be the servants of those (men and women) who will inherit salvation (1:14). Moreover, we are told that when one sinner repents and turns from sin, *"the Angels of God rejoice"* (Luke 15:10).

THE PLACE OF ANGELS IN THE ORDER OF CREATION

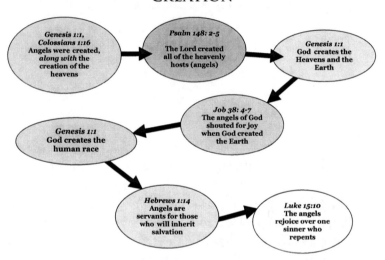

ANGEL QUIZ: ANSWERS

1	People become Angels when they die.	False	Lk. 20:24-36
2	Angels are chubby naked babies.	False	Daniel 8:15ff;
3	Michael the Archangel and Jesus are one and the same.	False	Hebrews 1:5; II Peter 1:17
4	Satan is a Fallen Angel.	True	Isa. 14:12; Ezek.28:12)19
5	Angels have bodies like humans.	False	Ps.104:4; Heb.1:14
6	There are more Angels than there are people.	True	Heb.12:22; Rev. 5:11
7	Angels reproduce.	False	Lk.20:34-36
8	Angels can be killed.	False	Lk.20:34-36
9	Children are assigned guardian Angels at birth to watch over them.	False	Matthew 18:10 / Acts 12:15
10	Hell was made for the devil and his fallen Angels.	True	Mth.25:41

11	Christian believers will judge Angels.	True	1 Cor. 6:3
12	Angels can take the form of men and women and walk among us.	True	Heb.13:2; Gen.19:1; Acts 8:26; Acts 12:7
13	Angels live on earth most of the time.	False	Lk.2:13-15; Gal.1:8; Jude 6
14	Angels can express emotions.	True	Hebrews 1:14; Luke 15:10
15	Angels live inside of and possess humans.	False	Lk. 1:15; 1:41; 1:67; Acts 7:55

WORKS CITED

Blue Letter Bible. "Book of Psalms 34 - (NLT - New Living Translation)." Blue Letter

Bible. 1996-2010. 24 Feb 2010. http://www.blueletterbible.org/Bible.cfm? b=Psa&c=34&t=NLT

Blue Letter Bible. "Book of Judges 6 - (NIV – New International Version)." Blue Letter

Bible. 1996-2010. 24 Feb 2010. http://www.blueletterbible.org/Bible.cfm?b =Jdg&c=6&t=NIV

Blue Letter Bible. "Revelation of Jesus Christ 19 - (NKJV - New King James Version)."

Blue Letter Bible. 1996-2010. 18 Mar 2010. http://www.blueletterbible.org/Bible.cfm?b=Rev&c=19&t=NKJV

Chafer, L. S. (1947). *Systematic Theology.* Dallas, TX: Dallas Texas Seminary Press.

Duffield, Guy P. & VanCleave, N.M. (1987). *Foundations of Pentecostal Theology.* San Dimas, CA: Life Bible College.

Easton, M.G. (1897). *Easton's Illustrated Bible Dictionary* (3rd Ed). Nashville, TN:Thomas Nelson Publishers, 1897.

Internet Movie Data Base. (1990-2010). Angel Movies. Retrieved from **Error! Hyperlink reference not valid.** find?s= all&q=angel+movies

Netflix. (1997-2010). *Angels.* Retrieved from http://www. netflix.com/MemberHome?lnkce=sntDd&lnkctr=mhb wse

The Holy Bible, New International Version. (1984). East Brunswick, NJ:International Bible Society.

ABOUT THE AUTHOR

Tracy Lewis, Ph.D. has been active in the ministry and in Christian Education for many years, serving in several different positions including Principal, Administrator, Youth Pastor, Youth Leader, Church Planter, Counselor. She currently serves as the Principal of Southpark Christian School, and as a part-time professor for Tulsa Community College in Tulsa, Oklahoma.

Dr. Lewis was born in Clarksburg, West Virginia but moved to Los Angeles, California at the age of 12. She became a Christian at the age of 16 at Maranatha Community Church in Los Angeles.

From 1988 to 1990 she attended Life Pacific College (Life Bible College) in California, then after joining the United States Air Force in 1990, she enrolled at Southeastern University in Lakeland, Florida and finished her Bachelor's Degree through distance education. In 1994 she moved to Virginia Beach, Virginia to attend seminary at Regent University. While pursuing her Masters of Divinity Degree, she worked as a graduate assistant administrator for the School of Divinity Dean's Office under Dr. Vinson Synan and Dr. Lyle Story. Dr. Lewis consecutively served as Youth Pastor and as a Young Life Leader in two different high schools while attending Regent University and received their Community Service of the Year Award upon graduation as well as the Who's Who in American Colleges and Universities Honor.

After graduating from Regent University in 1997, Dr. Lewis served at Mercy Ministries in Nashville, Tennessee. In 1999 she moved to Juneau, Alaska and went to work for the Information Technology Department for the State of Alaska. She returned to Virginia in 2001 and served for several years as a CASA (Court Appointed Special Advocate) for abused and neglected children and as a CASA supervisor. During this time, she also served as a Youth Pastor at her church.

In 2004, Dr. Lewis began working on her doctorate in education. From 2005 to 2007 she served on staff at St. Anne's-Belfield School in Charlottesville, Virginia. She moved to Tulsa, Oklahoma in 2007 to work for Tulsa Community College and also began working for Associated Centers for Therapy. Dr. Lewis completed her Ph.D. in Post-Secondary and Adult Education from Capella University, and in 2008 she simultaneously enrolled in the Graduate School of Education at Oral Roberts University and began taking classes in Christian School Administration.

Dr. Lewis ministry, studies, and desire to experience other cultures has taken her all over the U.S., including Alaska where she lived for almost five years, and even to Australia. She has a passion and respect for the Judeo-Christian Scriptures in their original languages, Greek and Hebrew. She has dedicated her life to the study and defense of the Greek language, theology, and biblical history. She also has a love for languages and speaks both modern Greek and Spanish. Dr. Lewis is also the author of *Identifying Ways to Increase Learner Persistence in GED Programs in the U.S.*

CPSIA information can be obtained at www.ICGtesting.com
Printed in the USA
LVOW12s0252250714

395982LV00011B/81/P